What Not To Post For Students

How to Use Social Media to Get Ahead

P.K. Renner

© 2013 Lucky Bluebird Press, author P.K. Renner

ISBN-13:
978-0615799520 (Lucky Bluebird Press)

ISBN-10:
0615799523

All Rights Reserved. No part of this publication may be reproduced in any form or by any means, including scanning, photocopying, or otherwise without prior written permission of the copyright holder.

First Printing, 2013 v1.0

Printed in the United States of America

Liability Disclaimer

By reading this book, you assume all risks associated with using the advice given below, with a full understanding that you, solely, are responsible for anything that may occur as a result of putting this information into action in any way, and regardless of your interpretation of the advice.

You further agree that our company cannot be held responsible in any way for the success or failure of you or your enterprise as a result of the information presented in this book. It is your responsibility to conduct your own due diligence regarding the safe and successful use of these practices if you intend to apply any of our information in any way to your own goals and aspirations.

Terms of Use

You are given single non-transferable, "personal use" license to this book. You cannot distribute it or share it with other individuals.

Also, there are no resale rights or private label rights granted when purchasing this book. In other words, it's for your own personal use only. DO NOT DUPLICATE.

For special discounted rates and free resources for schools and other organizations, visit www.whatnot2post.com.

What Not To Post For Students

How to Use Social Media to Get Ahead

For Elizabeth

Contents

Contents 7
Preface 11
   The SWAG Rules™ of Social Sharing 13
You Are Your Own Brand 15
   Examples of Personal Brands 16
   The Internet is a Mirror 18
      Somebody's Watching You 19
"Who Cares What I Do Online?" 21
   Key Points to Remember 26
   People Who Care 27
      College Admissions Staff 27
      People Who Might Hire You 30
      People in Select Programs 35
      People Who Want to Give You Money 36
      Those Closest to You 39
   Identifying "Who Cares" 41
Developing Your Own Personal Brand Online 45
   People as Products 47
      Step One: You, Through Your Own Eyes 48
      Step Two: You, Through the Eyes of Others 50
      Step Three: Looking Forward 51
      Step Four: Building Your Brand 55
Tools for Building Your Online Brand 57
   Facebook 58
   Twitter 59
   LinkedIn 60
   Snapchat 61
   Pinterest 62
   Vine 63

- Google+ 63
- Instagram 64
- Tumblr 64
- Myspace 65

What NOT to Post 67
- What's at Stake 69
  - Talking Trash 69
  - Bad to the Bone 70
  - Red Solo Cups 71
  - Weapons of Mass Consumption 72
  - Let Me Be "Blunt" 73
  - My So-Called Life 74
  - Nasty Sign Language 75
  - Your Birthday Suit 76
  - Pink Flamingos in the Pool 76
  - Bad Language 77
  - TMI on PDA 78
  - Identity Details 78
  - False Friends 79
  - Don't be a Hater 80
  - Avoid Controversy 80
  - Stop Complaining 81
- A List of Don'ts, and other Best Practices 82
  - Security Concerns 84
- Cyber-Bullying, Shunning and More 86
- Why Your Posts Matter 87
  - Leading a Double Life 87
  - Time to Get Busy 88
- A Note for Protective Parents 89

Your Online Reputation 90
What to Post 95
- Your Amazing Talents 95
- Your Team Together 96
- Your Artistic Genius 97
- Your High Notes 98

8

- Your Best Dressed 99
- Your Outdoor Fun 100
- Your Wild Destinations 101
- Your Curtain Call 102
- Your Teen Spirit 103
- Your Best... 104
- Your Not-So-Best 105
- Your Awards and Honors 106
- Your Leadership 107
- Your Kindness to Others 108
- Your Community Service... 109
- Your Science Fairs and Mathletes 110
- Your Creative Talents... 111
- Your Groups and Gatherings....................................... 112
- Your Hard Work 113
- Your Friendships and Fun 114
- Your Hobbies and Passions 115
- Your Family Fun 116

10-Step Social Media Checklist 117
  Other Tips 119
Personal Brand Management 121
  Manage your Settings... 122
  Create a Roadmap for Your Reputation 123

Preface

"Whatever! I can post what I want. It's no big deal. Nobody cares what I have to say anyway."

Oh, such a sad statement made by a naive 15 year old. Little does she know that within a few months, her posts and online activity will come back to haunt her. But with a little luck and strategic direction, her choice of topics shared could actually transform her future.

You already know how to use social media. The purpose of this book is to help you use it better – to think about the big picture as you share small things. If you're a student in junior high, high school or college, *What Not To Post* is designed to give you a clear advantage when it comes to standing out and getting what you want. Vying to get accepted into a competitive program? Trying to get that exclusive internship – or at least get your foot in the door for an interview? This short book contains the tools you need to design a roadmap to help get you there – or at least secure a stronger position in the running.

Never before have students had such opportunity to express themselves in such vivid detail. In 140 characters or less, each day brings new opportunity to tell the world what they think, what matters most to them, and who they are as individuals. Their thoughts, their feelings, their ambitions, their likes and dislikes – all of it pours out of their heads and on to the pages of Facebook, Twitter, Pinterest, Instagram, and other social sites yet to come. It's not only how we stay connected with one another in our professional and personal lives, social media is how we share our stories.

Everybody has a story. Pick a name and Google it. See what comes back in the results, and what it says about them, and those who share their same name. Your story may already be out there on the Internet. So, what does your "social story" say about you?

For many of us, Facebook and Twitter (even Snapchat and Instagram) are part of our daily lives, woven into the fabric of how we engage with others, sharing what we experience. Beyond mere entertainment, social sites hold real power to raise the awareness of serious issues. A few well-planned tweets can topple regimes, as in Egypt's Arab Spring. What you have to say can catch fire and inspire real change in the world. Your keystrokes can do more than simply reply to your friends. You can use them to share the joy of personal achievements, to teach, to inform and to entertain. Your access to social media channels offers you free, instant reach to broadcast in-the-moment news, personal reflection, inspirations, fresh ideas – even cute kitty pictures – in the blink of an eye, tap of a screen or the click of a mouse.

For students and teens, this opens up an incredible opportunity for those savvy enough to take advantage of it. Instead of letting life happen to you and taking a passive approach to your online persona, the pages to follow will help you understand what not to post, good things to share, ways to use specific social media tools, and how to build your online story. Instead of using social media to simply connect with friends and family, now you can use it to your advantage.

The SWAG Rules™ of Social Sharing

If you're going to share, share with swag! Here are the SWAG Rules of Social Sharing. Keep SWAG in mind before you post.

S: Smart – Is this a smart thing to share? Does it advance my goals, or could it cause problems for me in the future if the wrong people read it? Could I get in trouble for sharing this, or will my choice of words offend someone – especially if I poke fun at another person? Think it through and decide if this post makes you look good, or whether or not it's a very smart thing to say.

W: Wholesome – Is it PG-13? Is this a good thing to post, or will it cause harm to my reputation or to the reputations of others? Is it friendly teasing, or is it crossing the line into bullying? Does it give people the wrong idea about me? If the things you post are not wholesome or in good taste, it just makes you look bad. When in doubt, leave it out.

A: Authentic – Does this reflect who I am as a person? Is this how I want others to perceive me? Is this an accurate reflection of myself? Be true to who you are. Share your best with others. Whether you are building a personal brand online or just having fun connecting with friends, be yourself.

G: Grandma Test – Would you want your grandma to read this, or another adult who is important to you whose opinion you value? Would you feel ashamed of yourself or embarrassed if they saw it? If it doesn't pass the Grandma Test, then don't use it.

You Are Your Own Brand

Like it or not, everybody has a reputation. We all are evaluated and labeled by everyone we meet – in school, at church, at the mall, in real life, and especially online. You've already heard that saying, "You never get a second chance to make a first impression." Well, it's certainly true when it comes to building up your online reputation and personal brand.

You probably don't consider yourself to be a "hater" and you might not believe in labels. Maybe you believe stereotypes are unfair, that we all are unique individuals worthy of independent and fair evaluation. Perhaps you feel like people just need to spread more love instead of judging each other all the time. That's nice, but it's not about what you think – it's about what others think of you. Frankly, this is a fact of life that you can leverage to your advantage.

We humans are wired for groups. We live in communities. We travel in packs. We belong to cliques or clubs. It is part of our nature to identify and categorize others. Friend or foe? Funny or annoying? Helpful or hurtful? Labels and stereotypes are how all people process and store information about the people they encounter. Our brains like to put people in boxes or groups so we know what to expect from them, and how we can anticipate them to act when we have to deal with them again in the future.

Of course, people are good at judging others, but how they judge you does not have to be negative. It's natural to take in information and process that information through the lens of our experiences, to form opinions about an individual. Those initial opinions set the tone for our online reputation. This is the initial critical element of your personal brand.

Businesses know how to manage the opinions people may form about their products and services. This is called marketing. Companies spend billions of dollars each year to present a specific image and message to people, in the hopes of influencing them to buy their product or to think highly of their work. How they package the marketing message – from colors used on their packaging to the models in their ads to the size of the logo on their product – all come together to create their brand. It's like a mosaic – hundreds of details come together to create a specific experience for the customer to enjoy. A brand is the emotional and psychological relationship or connection the product or company has with its customers. Some brands bring out strong opinions, emotions, and sometimes can even evoke physiological responses from customers.

Think about how you feel when you wear a name-brand shoe, like Nike®, as compared to the no-name brand your mom came home with on sale. Let's compare the two. Both shoes fit. Both look good. But chances are you'll want to "Just Do It" and spend the extra $40 for the swoosh on the side. Nike is just one example. You can check your closet for dozens more.

Examples of Personal Brands

People can be brands as well. Consider how sports personalities can be more like products than athletes. Former high-school basketball prodigy LeBron James became a brand at an early age, with sponsors watching his evolution to superstar. Unfortunately, his hometown hero image when playing for the Cleveland Cavaliers went up in smoke after his hour-long ESPN special announcing his move to the Miami Heat. The fallout and public outrage over that one moment transformed LeBron from everyone's favorite player to one of the most hated players in the league. It tarnished his personal brand (some would say destroyed it), costing him millions of dollars in sponsorship deals. He has since recovered somewhat, but he still doesn't have the endorsement power he once enjoyed.

Another example is Justin Bieber. His image strikes an emotional response in people. Some people love him (Bieber Fever!). Others despise him. Some even claim to become physically ill when they hear his music. He started out as a regular kid with some great cover songs on YouTube, was discovered, and quickly became a teen icon. Love the Beebs or not, he's a great example of personal branding. From his unique hairstyles to the random topics he tweets, you know what you're going to get – what to expect – in the brand-fan relationship.

President Obama is another example of personal branding for success. Back in 2006, this junior senator from Illinois had bigger things in mind. He assembled an awesome team of marketers and together they built an irresistible campaign approach. This included consistent messaging ("Yes we can!"), a logo design exclusive to him, a massive email list to solicit campaign contributions and to rally support, and an overreaching strategy that landed him exactly where he wanted to be – leader of the free world! While some may not agree with his politics, most will agree that his ability to create a super strong personal brand is admirable. In fact, even before he won the election in 2008, his team won Ad Age magazine's "Marketer of the Year" award, recognized for using social media and online strategies to go from being virtually unknown to becoming the President of the United States.

LeBron, Justin Bieber and Mr. President all found success by developing a personal brand that aligns with their ambitions. You can do the same, and the easiest way to get started is with the strategic use of social media.

The Internet is a Mirror

What you do online reflects who you are as an individual. In fact, think of your computer or smartphone screen as a mirror that reflects your life – your thoughts, activities and interests come together to create an image. So if you were to go back through your posts, threads and shares online, what type of person do you see reflected in the choices made?

People often define integrity as doing the right thing when no one is watching. This holds true when you use social media. What you do, say and search for on the Internet may be more public than you may realize. If you logged into a shopping site using your Facebook account, for instance, the items you browse could end up posted on your wall. Sign up for Spotify through your Facebook account, and the songs, titles and artists you listen to are shared with the world. Privacy settings and preferences can help manage how much is shared, but this may be more a benefit than an annoyance. The sooner you understand that your online life is transparent and the items you choose to post really do matter, the sooner you can start developing a rock-solid online personal brand to serve you for years to come.

Somebody's Watching You

Does it sound creepy that people who you don't even know might be checking you out online at this very moment? We use the tools that are available to us. Before the Internet, if a person wanted information, they went to the phone book. Today they use search engines and Facebook. What do you do when you want to learn more about a person? Chances are you search for them on Twitter, Instagram or Facebook.

By understanding the way people seek out information, you can better manage the details about you that exist online. As much as you may think this doesn't matter (or that you're too young to care about what people think), your future self would probably be a little annoyed with your current self for having that attitude. In fact, your future self could be suffering and stuck, all because of the bad decisions your current self makes today – especially with what you do online.

Think about it for a moment – consider what your friends say on Twitter. Funny comments... cruel observations... ridiculous shares – it's certainly entertaining! But what happens when your friend's future self – whose life-long dream is to be a child-rights advocate and attorney – is trying to get an internship at a prestigious law firm. It's a huge opportunity. She has a great chance, but it's extremely competitive. A family friend at the firm tells her that she's one of two finalists. She couldn't be more excited.

The human resources (HR) person at the law firm has to help the internship coordinator with the tough decision between the two candidates. Because HR is in charge of finding the best and brightest person for the position, he decides to check Facebook, Twitter and LinkedIn to get a better idea of the person behind the application. After a quick search, he finds a rich history of your friend's toxic comments. "Oh, she's good on paper, but this one could be a real liability for the firm. If she's anything like her Twitter feed, she's way too risky. Let's go with the other person who seems a bit more steadfast."

Poof! Your friend's glowing chances at a life-changing opportunity quickly disappear. Your friend lost out because she failed to properly manage her personal brand.

Consider this: If an outside person who matters to you (or to your future) checks you out online, what type of person will be looking back at them? When you start thinking of the Internet as a mirror, you can begin to control your reflection. Your public persona can be easily enhanced once you get a strategy in place, which will be explained in detail in the pages that follow. But before we work on strategy, let's first look at who cares, why it matters and why you need to design a personal brand that works best for you that supports your ambitions.

"Who Cares What I Do Online?"

The following is a true story. The names and some details have been changed to protect their identities.

For most of her life, Mary lived in her brother's shadow. It was true when they were children, and even more apparent once they got to high school.

"Oh, so you're Mark's little sister? Wow, he's a great guy."

"I had Mark in my class two years ago. I expect great things from you, Mary, if you're anything like your brother."

"Well, if your brother can get straight A's while playing football and working at the pizza shop a few days a week, I'm sure you can at least do as well, considering you're not even playing soccer this season."

Mary pushed herself every day. The homework that took the "smart kids" like her brother an hour to do took her two, but she plowed through it. She was determined to show them that she was just as good – maybe even better. She always did the best she could not to disappoint anyone.

When Mary got accepted into her first-choice college, she was beyond elated. She was determined to work even harder to get into her program, which was her life-long dream.

Ever since she broke her leg while snowboarding while in middle school, she wanted to be a biomedical engineer, to develop new technologies to support neuromuscular advancements for young athletes. Her college had one of the best the engineering programs in the country. She knew she could make a difference to help student athletes to recover from injury even faster. Maybe she would be nationally recognized for her advanced procedures. Imagine all the people she could help and the lifestyle she would enjoy!

But the first step was to get into the right college, which she did. The second step would come after her first year when she would apply for acceptance into the university's biomedical engineering program. Because only a limited number of applicants are accepted, Mary was determined to do whatever it took to get in.

That summer after high school graduation, she volunteered three days a week in the orthopedic wing of the local children's hospital. Not only did she love helping the kids, she also wanted to make sure she had community service that aligned with her passion to get into that program. She also helped out as an assistant coach with the youth soccer program at church.

After her shifts and practices, she spent as much time as possible with her high school friends, celebrating graduation all summer long, knowing they'd all be leaving each other soon. Even though they were off to different colleges in different cities, they made a vow to keep in touch on Twitter, Instagram and Facebook. BFFs to stay BFFs.

In August, Mary was in the parking lot of her new dorm, nervously waving goodbye to her parents as they pulled away. It was the first time she was on her own, a fresh start at a new life – her own life. Tears turned to smiles, fear to relief. No more parents around telling her what to do… nobody comparing her to her perfect brother… no one pushing her to do better, to be better. For the first time, she was in control of her destiny. It felt good.

However, that good feeling quickly faded. By the end of that first month at college, Mary was not speaking to her roommates ("They are so lame – all they do is study all the time and yell at me to be quiet when I come home at night. Total losers.") She found new friends, who she called her "study group." They lived on the floor below, and soon that is where she spent most of her time. With her study group, she made good use of her older cousin's driver's license, supplying the beer for tailgating and pregame parties. (Her fake friends loved her fake ID.) She started "studying" a new band, even traveled on weekends to other cities to hear them play. She got a tattoo, pierced her tongue, gained 15 pounds and was living the dream, or so she thought. Soon that new freedom would break her heart.

In high school, Mary was considered a "try-hard," or someone who had to work twice as hard to get the same grades as those more gifted. She was supported by a network of friends, family and teachers who encouraged her success – who helped her stay focused. Now that she was in college, her new network (aka "study group") was less concerned about her success and more concerned about having a good time. Weekend parties bled into Thursdays… then into Wednesday "hump day" celebrations. But she made it a rule to always get her work done before she went out. Even if she had to bring her book to study group while the music was blasting, she did what she had to do to keep up. Her real dream, though dim, was still there. She really needed to do well this semester to even have a chance at getting into the biomed program.

Keeping in touch with her friends back home was easy. Mary loved to tweet about the crazy things she was doing, sharing pictures on Facebook and Instagram. She made sure that picture after picture, post after post, told them what a good time she was having – from tailgating toasts of red Solo cups raised high, to almost passing out in the piercing parlor with her tongue sticking out, to smoking with her study group on Wednesday nights. Finally, out from under the grip of her parents' rules, she wanted to show what her life was really like – a big party! Fun, right?

Here's the issue. What Mary didn't realize is that people beyond her group of friends were very interested in what was going on with her life. From her church elders (who provide scholarship dollars for her to attend college) to her parents (who want to be proud of her) to the hospital administrators (where she hopes to get a paid internship after working for free all last summer) to the owner of the pizza shop (where she may have to apply for a job to help with expenses) to the admissions director of the college of engineering (who has to sift through 1,078 applicants vying for just 50 spots available in the program) – all of these people are interested in how Mary is doing. Who is she? What's she up to? What matters to her most? What type of person is she beyond the formal application and essays?

DISCUSSION:

1) When you think about Mary's situation, do you think what she shared online helped her chances at getting into her program (or for her job, or for her scholarship to renew), or do you think she will wind up hurting herself and her chances?

2) If you were an admissions director, do you think you would select Mary for your top-notch program based on your impression of her from what you could see online?

3) What do you think Mary should do to fix her situation, and/or help her chances in the future?

Key Points to Remember

Before going further, keep these two truths in mind.

1) Privacy settings are a joke. Don't trust them and don't count on them to protect you. Yes, they may prevent your Aunt Nosey from snooping around your wall, but anyone with a vested interest in finding out more about you (such as human resource professionals who hire you, admissions professionals who accept you, scholarship boards who review you, athletic coaches who recruit you, etc.) can find back doors into your online world and see what's really going on in your personal life. Posts and pictures are shared. Even Twitter can reveal your secrets when followers re-tweet what was once private. If you do prefer to use your settings to block others from seeing what you post, be vigilant about maintaining your security. (Sign out and test it from time to time.) Platform settings change so often that the best way to keep up with online privacy is to be smart about what you post to begin with.

2) The Internet writes in ink. I'll say it again, posts can be permanent. Even if you take it down, there are tech-savvy who people can access what once was there. Before you share, be sure it's not something you'll want to take back later. Even Snapchat with its little ghost could come back to haunt you.

Now that we have those two points covered, let's talk about who's looking at you online, and what you can do to make sure your first impression is a good one once they find you.

People Who Care

Social media offers many tools of perception. You can use Facebook, Twitter and other outlets to shape how you are perceived by those interested in learning more about you.

The Internet is your canvas, and your posts are the brushstrokes of your self-portrait – how people see you online. Let's explore who might care what you do online and what they might be looking for when searching for details about you and your life.

College Admissions Staff

When a student applies to a college, it's as if they're sending out a personal invitation to college staff (admissions, coaches and/or program coordinators) to judge and evaluate them. Your grades, standardized test scores, "permanent record" of school behavior, attendance records, extra-curricular activities, leadership recognition, volunteer service hours – all of these things (and more) go in to make up your official profile. The specific details that factor into any admissions review vary in importance from one school to the next. But one element that's becoming more widely used by admissions officers to explore an individual's background (and their character) is social media – especially Facebook and Twitter.

Since grade school, your teachers have been telling you that character counts. So what kind of character are you? Many colleges don't look at grades alone. Some look for the type of individuals who could enhance the existing student body. They want a blend – a mix of students with a range of abilities and talents. Too many athletes or too many artists in one class can change the reputation of the school and what it's known for, so schools make conserted efforts to have a diverse group of individuals for each freshman class. To accomplish this mix, it requires them to dig beyond the transcripts and test scores. They need to get to know the students as individuals. In-person interviews are important, but schools are also looking to social media and the Internet as recruitment and admissions tools.

The most often used tool is Facebook. Even if you find Facebook boring, don't ignore it entirely. Facebook has become a highly valuable resource for admissions staff who want more background details on applicants. Each year, more and more universities report that they look at the Facebook pages of applicants. Many use Facebook as a tool of introduction, to get to know them better before meeting them in person for admissions interviews. It's not about "checking up" on you. It's really more about getting to know who you truly are as a person beyond your application and essay.

Is this fair game? Sure it is! Everything you put online that is accessible to the public is fair game, and could be considered public information. If your information is not protected by privacy settings, you open yourself up. If your settings allow people to see a photo that is less than appropriate, that's your problem – not theirs. Or if a Twitter search for your name reveals a series of rants or comments you made using f-bombs and other vulgar language, again, that's your problem.

Many of the images (both good and bad) used in this book and on WhatNot2Post.com are taken directly from social media accounts of people who have lousy privacy settings. It's amazing the type of things you can find when you search for random names or friends of friends, and click through to their photos. (How to manage your photo privacy settings will be explained later in this book.)

It's a good bet that many applicants to top-tier schools who were strong on paper ended up quietly losing the opportunity for admissions because of Facebook posts and photo tags – even when the questionable photos of the individual were posted and tagged by someone else. Alcohol in photos, underage drinking, racist jokes or hate speech – even something as "simple" as teasing sarcasm (or worse yet, bullying) on a comment thread – all can result in you losing your opportunity to your first-choice colleges before you even get to the interview. All you'll get is a standard rejection letter and an empty feeling over what could have been.

Admissions professionals may claim to reject the use of social media as part of the formal process; however, many use it to see if the person is a "good fit" for the university. As we mentioned earlier, when schools seek out a certain type of individual – one who has the personality and the attitude that will add to (and benefit) the current mix of students – their evaluation may include a quick search on social media. An online persona can directly reflect a person's values, interests, background, disposition, and other core qualities that may help admissions predict whether or not you will enhance the campus community in a positive way. That is why it is important for students to be thoughtful about what they post. We'll get into more detail on this in the pages ahead.

NOTE: Be aware that this is a two-way street. Not only are colleges using Facebook to get to know applicants better, they're also using it to allow those same applicants to know more about the university. Most universities (and even programs within) have some sort of presence on Facebook. For the colleges that interest you most, be sure to check them out. You can even like them, follow them, and share what they post or re-tweet what they share. This shows admissions leadership that you are interested and engaged in what they offer. If they're using social media for recruitment, use it to your advantage.

People Who Might Hire You

Research released by Reppler in early 2013 showed that 91% of employers turn to social media to screen applicants, and 76% of those look to Facebook before they hire someone.

Someday you'll need to get a job. Even if you don't want to go to college or you aren't interested in getting admitted to a competitive school, you will someday be interested in earning a living and working somewhere.

If you hope to be hired at a medium- or large-sized company, you have to get past the human resources department or HR. Part of the job of HR is to make sure the right people are in the right jobs. Sometimes they act as recruiters, searching

LinkedIn, Monster.com and other online resources to find people with a certain skillset to fill a specific job that opens up. Sometimes they take the people suggested or recommended by others to make sure they have the skills, attitude and aptitude required for the job.

HR professionals are the ones who prescreen potential applicants before interviews. Other times they're making sure the person who had a solid first interview is worth calling back in for the second round – or the job offer. Again, it's their responsibility to make sure people are the all-around best for the job. Their input can factor into how much you get paid (in salary or by the hour) for what you do. If the candidate for the job seems very impressive, HR may push for more money or other perks to make sure the deal is attractive enough to get that candidate to accept and come to work for them. And if the candidate is all talk with no real experience, HR may suggest a low-ball offer (or below what the job usually pays) or no offer at all.

So, how can you, as a young person with little real work experience, show these HR folks that you're worth every penny – and maybe even more? How can you show what you know from other life experiences when there's not a space for "life experience" on the application form? Building a strong online persona can help. We will explore ways to do that in the next chapter.

You can count on the fact that the person who coordinates job interviews and juicy offer letters will do what's called "due diligence" before hiring just anyone. That means they will check and double check the available history of the top choices for the job to make sure they are who they say they are, that their skills and background match up with what they said in the interview, and that they'll be a good fit within the organization.

Being a good fit means they'll fit in with other people and with the corporate culture of the organization. Corporate culture includes the type of working environment at a company and shared attitudes, interests and ethics (or corporate vision/mission) of those who work together. Some companies only look for specific skills. Others want people who have a certain vibe or attitude. Sometimes these things are hard to discover based on background check alone. Many times additional research (i.e., searching online) is required to be sure.

You might be surprised at the personal information people can access about you in a traditional background check. Most of it is part of the public record created by government agencies. Here's a short list of information typically included.

- Driving records

- Vehicle registration

- Credit records

- Criminal records

- Social Security number

- School records

- Court records

- Character references

- Neighbor interviews

- Medical records

- Drug test records

- Past employers

- Personal references

When you consider how a background check will read if the report is about you personally, you can see that the information is pretty limited. It may offer some official highlights, but doesn't even begin to provide the complete picture of you as a person, what interests you and your attitude toward life. But for many jobs, the law (state and/or federal) requires the employer to check the history of the people they hire. This is for the protection of those they serve. Jobs working with children, the elderly or people with disabilities are just some of the positions that will almost always require a criminal background check. But even if a background check isn't required, your future boss still wants to know who you are.

So, aside from pulling an official background check, what's the next best thing to get the details on a person? You Google them. You also search their name on various social sites. (Please note that even if you're using an alias name for your social media antics, you can still show up in search results if they know where to dig.)

Small businesses are the largest employers of young adults. Most small businesses don't have an official HR department, so they may skip much of the formal due diligence (like background checks) when they're looking to hire new people. Many business owners "go with their gut" when it comes to hiring. If their positive impression about a person after the interview is backed up by a strong application and glowing references, that used to be enough to get the job. But with such easy access to information online – personal information included – many small business owners and managers look to the Web to get a more complete story about those they're about to hire.

Your first job may seem beneath you or too basic, but that business was created because of the vision of its owner. Someone at some point had a dream, or they identified a need to serve others in exchange for enough money to make a profit. Small business owners are struggling today, and it's expensive to hire someone. It's even more expensive to hire the wrong person. Because of this, many will invest the extra time to dig a little deeper to find the real story behind the person sitting across from them asking for a job.

The fact that your future boss cares about who you are and what you do opens up a huge opportunity for you. Now you have the chance to make a strong first impression when people are introduced to you through online search and research. Later in the book we'll outline steps you can take to design an online presence that's natural and true to who you are, but also includes your best qualities – qualities your future employers would like to see so they can get to know you better. This will improve your chances at success.

People in Select Programs

Not every job you go after will be for pay. Many opportunities provide great learning and leadership opportunities without a paycheck attached; however, you still have to be accepted.

Volunteer Opportunities – Serving your community is one of the best things you can do to gain skills, meet people and simply give back. Volunteering just feels good. Plus, many schools require a number of service hours to graduate. Even organizations that work with volunteers (without paying them) can be selective in who they choose for their teams. Depending on the communities they serve, it's often standard practice to check out applicants before they are accepted to participate. Much like an employer, non-profits sometimes will go online to make sure you are who you say you are, and that you're the best person for the opportunity. Don't let your online antics and documented bad behavior harm your chances of gaining experience that could help you – and help others – in the future.

Societies, Clubs and Member Associations – No matter what field you're interested in for your career, chances are there is a membership organization or community connected with it. Member associations provide continuing education to those who join. They keep members updated on trends and techniques, and they show the world that their members have an active interest in advancing within that area of specialty. Association membership can be a valuable tool to enhance your online brand. It shows you're willing to do a little extra, that you're committed to your goals, and you make every effort to surround yourself with like-minded individuals in your field. You probably have membership organizations at your school that are more selective than others, such as National Honor Society or Key Club where your acceptance is decided upon by teachers or peers. Typically these groups want members who will enhance their image and advance their mission – not people who could damage a group's reputation in any way. Some groups offer excellent leadership opportunities and can truly enhance your overall high school experience. If you want in – or are the least bit interested in participating if asked – be sure your online image puts a good face forward to increase your likelihood of acceptance.

Internships – It's hard to get work experience when you don't have a job, and it's hard to get a job because you don't have any experience. Internships help break the cycle. These are typically unpaid, entry-level opportunities to work with companies, hospitals, or government agencies in return for real-life work experience and on-the-job training in a specific career area. You get great experience and something to put on your resume in return for little or no pay. Getting an internship is worth it. A successful experience can help you rise above the rest in career skills, references (people you can list on an application who will say good things about you), and solid life experience when applying for future opportunities. Because these opportunities are limited, those who decide on the individuals to take part will do a very thorough review of each prospect. Interviews, references, and applications are common. An online search could also factor into the selection decision, so it helps if your online image reflects some of the many reasons why you'd be perfect for the job.

People Who Want to Give You Money

At some point, you may want to apply for scholarships, grants and other funding to help you toward future projects and goals. This means you will fill out an application, compose an essay or even write a grant request that explains in earnest why you deserve the money – and why you'll make the best use of it. It could be as simple as applying for $100 from the "college help fund" at your church, to asking for consideration for a full ride to your favorite college, to requesting money for new playground equipment so the children in your community stay active.

The money you hope to receive is managed by people, typically several people who serve on a board or committee. They get dozens (perhaps even thousands) of requests, from people like you who also want their money. Their goal is to evaluate the person or group who will use their money to do something good with it, so their gift becomes an investment to make the world a better place. Different giving groups have different missions, but all of them want the money they give to do the most good.

Let's say there is grant money available for one high school student to study abroad in Copenhagen (Denmark) to learn about sustainable biofuel at the university as part of an international internship program. Hundreds of applications pour in from across the country. The decision makers on the board have narrowed the search to two people. Both applications appear to be outstanding. Both applicants scored high on the personal interviews and essay. Their references are equally strong. So, as a deciding factor, one of the board members goes online to learn more about the two finalists. He has some legitimate questions: Would each person will be successful living away from home for five weeks? Can they handle living in a different country? How responsible are they without constant supervision? Are they the best person for this opportunity without any potential for embarrassing the foundation providing the funding?

One look on Facebook and Twitter and the choice was clear.

Candidate B shared pictures of his Science Olympiad wins... his time spent last summer volunteering at the summer "Chem Camp" for kids at the local science museum... his backpacking trips and outdoor interests. He even posted and commented on an article about Chevron's new biofuel research, and another with his opinion on corn subsidies. This showed the board member that he was not only interested in the opportunity to study abroad – he was passionate about his goal of working in this industry.

Candidate A had been the leading candidate for consideration from the start. Her family was well connected; a local judge actually made a call to two board members with a personal reference, to put in a good word for her. Candidate A's scores were about even with Candidate B, but her essay was actually a little stronger. It was nice to see a young woman writing with such passion about biofuel research and global sustainability. Plus, they had never given a grant to a female student before. Her chances appeared to be very strong. That is, until they went online.

The board member started by searching her name in Google. It included a few mentions in the local paper for girls soccer, plus a few Twitter posts. He then checked her Facebook page. Most of her wall was private. Just a few profile photos were accessible. Most of those were of several young women at parties, arm in arm, clinging onto each other. One photo she was tagged in had a Jack Daniels bottle in the background – not good for a high school party. None of her "likes" included anything to do with school, her studies or her claims of interest in fuel research – just a few bands the board member had never heard of and some random humor blogs. Her Twitter posts were not easy to access, but a few were shared. In those she commented mostly on celebrity gossip, how bored she was with school, and her choice words about high school relationship issues.

Needless to say, the board member was no longer impressed. Candidate A's strong essay and family connections were not strong enough to overcome the damage she did to her own reputation online. As Candidate B packed his bags for this incredible opportunity, Candidate A was left behind, wondering what happened and tweeting about her disappointment.

Those Closest to You

Look around. You have so many people in your life who really care about you – who actively want to support your success, if you simply reach out and ask them for help. They care about you – and they care about what you do online. Many have invested their time, effort and energy to guide you. They want you to shine – to use your gifts to be your very best. Each of us has unique abilities and talents, but the opportunities for success can be limited – even sabotaged – by a careless approach to social media.

As we covered earlier, the Internet is like a mirror. It reflects the images that are put before it. Make sure your image online shines as the best representation of you – your interests, goals, hobbies, and friends. Only put your best self out there.

Of course, you can choose to ignore this advice; however, what you post today can and will impact your future, good or bad. It's better to set yourself up for success. Even small things you do to enhance your online image can go a long way when building a positive personal brand online. This becomes especially valuable when competing for opportunities against others who do nothing to protect or enhance their image online. The right approach can make you shine.

Identifying "Who Cares"

Here's a quick exercise. On each line below, list the names of two people within that category who believe in you, who want you to be successful. Even if you don't have an active relationship with each person you list, who do you think cares about your future. Also consider who you'd like to "make proud" or prove to them "you can do it" and achieve real success in life.

Teachers:

_____

_____

Coaches:

_____

_____

School Administrators and/or People at Church:

_____

_____

Family & Relatives:

_____

_____

Friends:

_____

_____

Next time you ask "Who cares what I do online?!" take a look at this short list above. I'm sure you can add more people to it. Your posts can impact your chances and opportunities with people you don't know and may never meet. But also know that what you do online also matters to those who care about you most.

Make them proud.

Extra Credit: Don't stop there. Think about your future goals and what you'd like to do once you've finished school. The people you will soon meet along your life's journey also matter.

Colleges You Like:

_____

_____

Places You'd Like to Work:

_____

_____

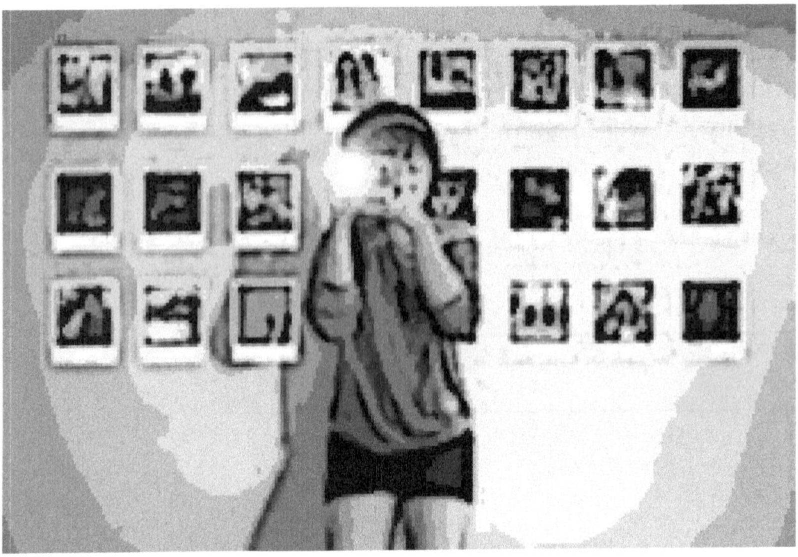

Developing Your Own Personal Brand Online

You are your own brand.

A personal brand is the image you project (both intentionally and unintentionally) about who you are and what you stand for. It's the details people see that bring about some type of impression. Even if you say "Don't judge" or "Don't be a hater," it's only natural for others to stereotype people based on their past experience with those who have similar qualities.

Some pre-existing prejudices are difficult to predict and can be challenging to overcome when people are considering you for an opportunity. You need to take a proactive approach to minimize any concern or potential issues. Instead of complaining about being the victim of stereotypes that you didn't personally create, instead do something positive to bring about real change.

For instance, there may be aspects of your online persona that can work against you, especially if you're unaware of the image you're putting out there. Designing a personal brand is not about being fake – it's about having an awareness of how your actions and activities may be perceived by others.

As mentioned in the previous chapter, your personal brand online can serve as a shortcut to that first impression you have with others – especially those evaluating you for admissions, scholarship awards, jobs, etc. That's why it's so valuable to take a thoughtful approach to the way you act, what you post, and how you present yourself through social media.

Everyone has an image. Look around your classroom. There are the jocks, the cheerleaders, the band rats, the smokers, the sweet, the geeks, the "too good for you's," the brains, the goths, etc. Why do people typecast others into these roles? It is how we naturally process information we perceive. Good person or bad person, fight or flight, worthwhile or worthless – all of these opinions speed our ability to make decisions and move forward toward our own needs.

Your online persona also will be stereotyped. You are creating an image with what you post. If someone today (who doesn't know you) took a look at the "you" online, what image would they see? That's where your personal brand comes into play.

Let's say the manager of your favorite retail shop is going through a stack of 87 applications for one job opening. You were born to work there – you love that store! She narrows the stack down to 10 people, but she only has time for five interviews. Chances are good that she will sort the stack based on what's on paper, then narrow her list by checking people out online and call the ones she likes best in for the interviews. If you're properly managing your online reputation and personal brand, you can improve the odds in your favor. If you really are perfect for that job, your personal brand should reflect that.

So let's look at how to design your own brand and establish a more positive "you" online.

People as Products

Think about the last time you went shopping for your favorite brands. Why do you like those specific brands so much? What is it about each that keeps you coming back for more?

A month ago, my friend needed a lightweight jacket. I found a nice one at the mall for him in the right size, color and design that he had described – and it was on sale. But when I gave it to him, he hated it – it wasn't what he wanted at all. Why? Because it didn't have "The North Face" logo on the shoulder. Brand was more important to him than value. In this case, the brand carried a positive image of quality, affluence, style, and outdoor adventure.

Brand also creates an emotional attachment. The reasons may not be rational but they exist. Consider the Starbucks daily devotees who can't start their day without seeing the green mermaid smiling back at them... Mac people versus PC people... Trader Joe's or Whole Foods versus family grocery stores... etc. Each brand carries with it a certain emotional connection so people know what to expect and how to feel when they use the product.

People are not much different, which is why it's important to use this basic instinct to your advantage. Your personal brand can leave others with the reassurance that you are the best person for the job or opportunity – or inform them enough about the "real you," so they're able to make their decision with confidence.

As mentioned earlier, when people meet, they process information about the person in front of them through the lens of their past experiences as they form opinions about that individual. The same is true when people "meet" you online. While checking out your social media presence and activities, they form opinions based on your image. Those opinions contribute to your reputation in the minds of others.

The real question is: What do you want to be known for?

Before you can answer that, you need to be clear on where you want to go – your goals, ambitions and objectives. These will directly influence the "you" that you put out there.

First, let's figure out who you are and how you would like to be perceived. Then we can map out how to put your best face forward to the world. We will also walk through the steps of designing a personal brand that best reflects the fabulous person you are.

Step One: You, Through Your Own Eyes

Who are you? What are your skills, abilities, and experiences that shape the person you are today? List your top three for each.

1) _____

2) _____

3) _____

What are your passions? List three things you feel strongly about. This passion often fuels aspects of our personality and helps to define a strong personal brand.

1) _____

2) _____

3) _____

What's unique about you? "Nothing" is not an acceptable answer. List three things that are special to you, your unique talents. What are your gifts worth sharing?

1) _____

2) _____

3) _____

Step Two: You, Through the Eyes of Others

How do others see you? What impression do you give to others when they meet you? What do your friends say about you? If you're not sure, send a text to five close friends and tell them you're doing a workshop and need them to share five adjectives to describe the person you are. Also, ask them why they chose the words they used. List the five words you think suit you best here:

1) _____

2) _____

3) _____

4) _____

5) _____

How are you perceived by those in authority? What might your teachers, coaches, and other people have to say about you? How would they describe you? If you're too shy to ask for their opinion directly, look back on report cards, conferences, and reviews to get an idea. List a few descriptive words here:

1) _____

2) _____

3) _____

What's your online reputation? Google yourself (search using your full name) and see what others are saying about you. (We'll get into reputation management soon.) What things would you like to improve about the results that came up?

1) _____

2) _____

3) _____

Step Three: Looking Forward

Have your goals in mind. Reflect for a moment: What you want out of life? What do you hope to accomplish once you graduate (or before)? What are your goals? Who is it you need to influence? Who might help you along the way? Who can help you get where you want to go? Take a moment and list your one-month, six-month, one-year, and five-year goals. List three for each timeframe.

ONE-MONTH GOALS: "In the next few weeks, I'd like to…"

1) _____

2) _____

3) _____

SIX-MONTH GOALS: "In the months ahead, I'd like to…"

1) _____

2) _____

3) _____

ONE-YEAR GOALS: "By this time next year, I'd like to…"

1) _____

2) _____

3) _____

FIVE-YEAR GOALS: "Once I finish school, I'd like to…"

1) _____

2) _____

3) _____

FUTURE SELF: "I want to be known for…"

1) _____

2) _____

3) _____

Who is the audience for your personal "brand"? If you're trying to get into a certain college or program, it may be the admissions director or program director. If you're trying to score an internship, it may be your advisor or the contact person at the place you hope to work. Once you understand and define your audience, it'll be easier for you to play up your strengths in the areas they may be looking for.

TARGET AUDIENCE:

1) _____

2) _____

3) _____

What's your style? Are you more of a laid-back yogi or a goal-driven high-achiever? Are you a comedian who loves to laugh, or are you more serious and to the point? We all wear masks. We all have different sides of ourselves to share with some, but not with others. Personalities can be like prisms. Think about which facets would be best to share with those you hope to influence, the target audience you just listed above.

Be sure your communications, posts and other online activity reflects who you are as a person. Also, be aware of those you just listed in the previous question and try to share things they'd like to see more of. Once you figure that out, be consistent and clear in your "voice" and choice of content. Switching off from cheerleader-spunky one day to Gothic-depressive the next sends mixed messages to people.

THREE QUALITIES OF YOUR PERSONAL STYLE:

1) _____

2) _____

3) _____

Above all, be authentic and keep your best face forward more often than not. That said, jot down the names of three people who are most similar to the person you hope to become. Think about others who have already found success in the fields that interest you – those who have already reached the same goals you've established for yourself. Look to them for design inspiration as you make decisions that may impact your personal brand. When in doubt, ask yourself, "What would _____ do?"

SUCCESSFUL PEOPLE YOU ADMIRE:

1) _____

2) _____

3) _____

Step Four: Building Your Brand

By now you have a better idea of who you are, what you want, who can help you, and what face you'd most like the world to see.

Just as the fashion industry can touch up the flaws to enhance what you see, savvy students can design a social media approach to make them more appealing and reinforce any perceived weaknesses. It starts with developing a strong personal brand.

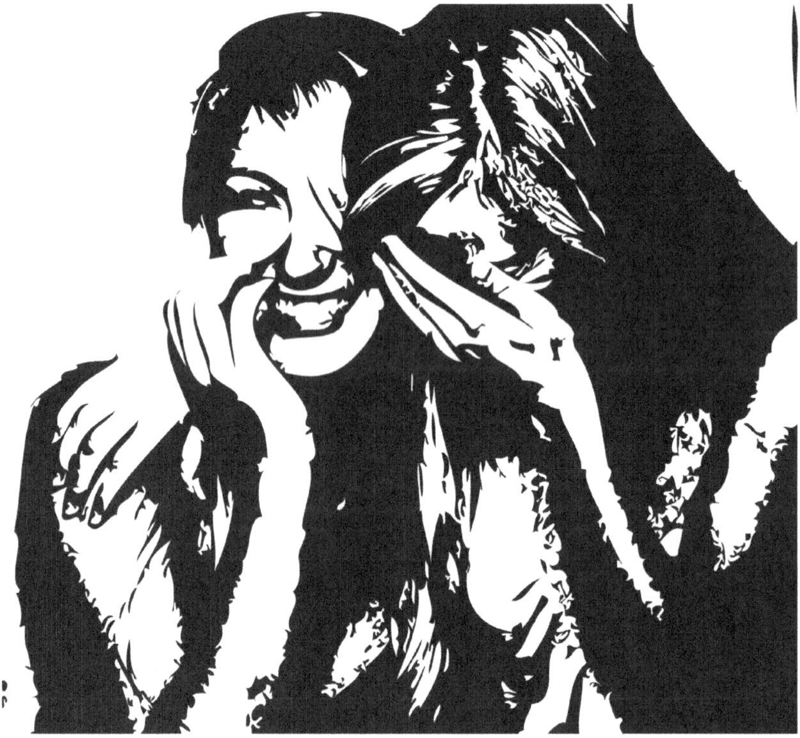

Tools for Building Your Online Brand

The best and brightest young people are no longer limited by geography or luck when it comes to becoming "known." All you need is an Internet connection to put yourself out there, gaining influence and notoriety beyond the confines of the community where you live. Of course, this can be both good and bad. The trick is to use your online activities to your advantage, creating an online image that can benefit you as you move toward your goals.

What seems like a few short years ago, your reputation or image was limited to your local community, based on things like your hobbies, your volunteer activities, your family's status, your job, how well you did in school, who you hang out with, etc. While most of that remains true, it's even more important to craft your story while protecting your image through social media.

Here are the social media platforms and options to consider and how you might use them to give you an edge, to help you stand out. Consider how each option can be leveraged alone or combined with others as you sculpt your image online.

With almost a billion members and growing, let's begin with Facebook.

Facebook

Facebook has evolved beyond a mere social network and into a vast and somewhat addictive digital community. Harvard Business Review describes it as "another World Wide Web, but with a profit motive." It has completely changed the way people connect with one another. In fact, you'd be hard pressed to go five minutes without seeing the blue "f" logo like image in print, on TV and online. Facebook dominates what we know as social media – anticipating nearly a billion users worldwide before the end of 2013 alone. To put this into perspective, that's one-eighth the population of the Earth. Here in the United States, about 10 percent of all time spent online is spent on Facebook. With so many active users, it's an obvious (and easy) place to start as you begin to carve your image online. Chances are good that after Google, it's the next place people will go to find more about you online. Even if you personally prefer other social sharing networks, Facebook matters most since it is most heavily used. Be sure to keep your profile somewhat active. While "Facebook fatigue" is growing and young people are bored and leaving, you still need to pay attention to Facebook as an important piece of your personal brand mosaic. Maintain your profile with care.

Twitter

Twitter is a nosy little bird, always interested in what's going on. It was designed to help friends, families and co-workers stay connected through short bursts of messages, 140 characters or less. These quick exchanges are designed around the answer to one simple question: "What are you doing?" Twitter users can post updates, "follow" other users to view their posts on a news feed, and even send public replies or private messages to connect with other tweeters. Over time tweets have evolved to include shared links to interesting content on the web, sharing ideas and opinions on hot topics (using # or hashtags), sharing photos, music, and more. Twitter happens to have excellent privacy settings, but they're not foolproof. Your tweets and comments can still find their way into search queries and other people's threads – people who have no privacy settings at all. Closing yourself off from others so they don't see what you're tweeting may not be the best approach. Instead, use Twitter the way marketers do. Share things that help establish you as a leader in your field of interest. Show that you're passionate about your work, your goals, and your life.

Twitter is also an excellent way to quietly become known by people who matter. If you really want to get that big job when you graduate, start following the company on Twitter. Find out who is in charge or who might be your boss and follow them as well. The same goes for college and university programs. Few things are more impressive during an interview than having the person say they've been following them on Twitter for several months – then cite a comment to praise or discuss. The old days of "need to know someone to get ahead" have been replaced with amazing access through social media. It's flattened the layers of society, making it easier than ever to find, reach and communicate with people from all levels of success. But before you start messaging people who matter, make sure the timing is right, and you have something of value to share.

LinkedIn

LinkedIn is like a Facebook for white-collar workers. The site describes itself as "the world's largest professional network with over 175 million members and growing rapidly." LinkedIn connects people to their trusted business contacts to exchange knowledge, ideas, and opportunities with a broader network of professionals. Basically, it's a website used by business professionals to connect with other professionals. It's also a valuable recruitment tool for HR and job placement professionals. Having a profile on LinkedIn gives you an easy-to-manage way to promote yourself professionally – allowing members to digitally connect and socialize, forging business connections that otherwise would be tough to create. Plus, it's a great way to highlight your experiences, expertise and resume information to advance your ambitions. LinkedIn was actually designed around helping people better manage their online identities. When you Google yourself (we'll get to this shortly),

LinkedIn profiles rise to the top of the search results, helping you make a stronger first impression online – if you manage your content properly.

When should you set up a profile on LinkedIn? When your job search requires you to submit a resume for a position instead of completing a standard job application form, then it's time to join. It's not a place for joking around. Keep it professional.

Snapchat

Snapchat is a photo sharing app for mobile designed to make social media fun again. The trend of users being forced to manage an idealized personal image has "taken all of the fun out of communicating," according to founder Evan Spiegel. Instead, he devised an app where users can take ridiculous and/or compromising photos to send to a specific list of recipients. Once viewed, the image self-destructs and erases. Once you snap a photo or video, you can overlay it with text and colors, plus set a time of expiration. Snaps can be viewed between one and 10 seconds before going away. The image is then deleted from all devices and Snapchat's servers. Screenshots are allowed, but the sender will receive a message letting them know their Snap was captured.

Some people think this is the perfect vehicle for sexting or sharing scandalous images, but it's not. The Internet writes in ink, as do most apps. While the pictures disappear after 10 seconds, the record of who interacted with whom doesn't.

And if you have a USB cable and a computer, you can easily search your phone's temporary files and retrieve photos or videos sent via Snapchat. People can always take screen shots. Even if you know who did, they can always post those images somewhere else and tag you in the photo. Or they could take a photo of a photo (or a video of a video). It's not as private as you think. While Snapchat isn't exactly going to advance your online image, it's worth mentioning because it certainly could hurt you if used inappropriately.

Pinterest

Pinterest is a social media tool that's gaining some impressive popularity. Think of it as a digital magazine or scrapbook of the cool things its users find online. Its official mission: "Our goal is to connect everyone in the world through the things they find interesting. We think that a favorite book, toy, or recipe can reveal a common link between two people. With millions of new pins added every week, Pinterest is connecting people all over the world based on shared tastes and interests." Your career interests and passions can be well showcased using Pinterest, plus it's a beautiful way to share your goals – what you think is important – via your Pinterest boards. If you build a Pinterest page around a specific goal or career desire, share that page with people who may interview you. Make it easy for them to see your best self online.

Vine

Vine is a new social sharing app that lets users create 6-second long video clips on an infinite loop and then share them on Vine, Twitter, and Facebook. If you like to create quick, amusing video clips, this is a good way to share them. Consider using it to highlight your goals, to showcase your abilities, and to grab attention using video to help you stand out. While some students have actually been accepted into competitive schools after making a clever YouTube video for the admissions officers, Vine may be a great tool to offer a quick, fun glimpse of your interests to share with those who matter. Time will tell how this new platform will evolve.

Google+

Google Plus is a niche community of users and groups. Contacts and users are organized into "circles" so you can control what you're communicating into each circle to better manage your personal brand. There are video "hangouts" where you can videochat with others with more spontaneity than other systems. It also offers a profile and news feed for your posts so you can keep up. In many ways, Google

Plus is similar to Facebook but with better privacy, fewer users and more features. I don't think it should be at the center of your personal branding efforts (don't start giving recruiters only your Google+ links instead of Facebook when they ask, or they'll think you're pulling one over on them), but it's one more area to add to the overall mosaic of how you could be viewed online.

Instagram

Instagram is a free photo-sharing program (now owned by Facebook) that allows users to take a photo, apply a digital artistic filter to it (so you can turn the image to different tones and treatments), and then share it on a variety of social networking services like Facebook. It's another way to add positive posts to your Facebook timeline – ones that look really cool.

Tumblr

A bridge in the gap between the brevity of Twitter and the heaviness of a traditional blog, Tumblr is a micro-blogging service designed to easily share things like photos, music, videos and links versus lengthy text-based posts. It's easy to use and easily customized, so you can quickly showcase your images in a stylish way. A Tumblr site is great for highlighting a specific topic area, including your passions and hobbies.

Myspace

Myspace was one of the original social networks and has been reconfigured to celebrate and showcase the work of musicians and the music scene/culture, asking "Artists, bring your original music with you." Upon sign up, you can see the focus is on the arts – music, photography, design, creative writing, and so on. If you're interested in a career in the arts, this may be a good place to showcase what you do and connect with others.

Now that you know where to post, let's talk about best practices for using social media to get ahead.

Social Media Explained

- **t** I'm eating bacon
- **f** I like bacon
- **in** I have skills including eating bacon
- ✅ This is where I eat bacon
- **YouTube** Watch me eat my bacon
- 📷 Here's a vintage photo of my bacon
- **P** Here's a recipe with bacon
- **g+** I work for Google and eat bacon
- **CS** I'm listening to music about bacon

©COREY SMITH · coreysmith.ws

What NOT to Post

Most readers are probably familiar with people whose lives have been damaged by social media. You've heard the stories... Athletes who spend their entire careers preparing for their moment of glory are suddenly booted off the team because of a bad tweet... People losing their jobs for sharing inappropriate comments or showing insensitivity toward others... "Sexting" (gross!)... Students getting suspended or jailed after their crazy behaviors are captured and shared online. You can catch the latest examples and news about bad behavior (and good ideas) at www.whatnot2post.com.

Again, you shouldn't count on your privacy settings to protect you. They won't. You simply need to take a proactive role to make sure you're managing your online image properly, using your social media activity to give you a real advantage when it counts.

As mentioned earlier, people will check you out online. Knowing this, you need to be aware of the "you" that you're presenting and make sure it's the representation you want to exist out there.

Always remember that there are consequences for the things you post and comment on. Those consequences can be good, or they can be bad – it's up to you. Right or wrong, fair or unfair, you will be judged in the future by the things you say today (and yesterday) online.

(Image credit: Astoria, Oregon Police Dept.)

This teenager in Oregon was driving home from a New Year's Eve party, hit two parked cars, and then joked about it on Facebook. Police caught up with him on New Year's Day and arrested him.

This is a classic example of what NOT to post.

Jacob Cox-Brown
2 hours ago

Drivin drunk... classsic ;) but to whoever's vehicle i hit i am sorry. :P

(Image credit: Facebook)

What's at Stake

Although you might not lose every opportunity based on your social media missteps, it might raise concern for colleges and future employers about the type of person you are and the quality of your character. You never get a second chance to make that first impression – and that includes the impression people have of you based on what they see online. If you do make the cut (even though there may have been damaging things discovered), you might be starting from behind. You're beginning a new stage in your life with a stain on your otherwise pristine image. It puts you at a disadvantage from day one, and you might not even learn why things seem so much harder for you until it's too late.

To fix that situation, let's start with some preventative maintenance. In the pages that follow are some specific things schools, parents and future employers DO NOT want to see in your posts, pins and tweets. Many of these suggestions will seem like common sense or just plain obvious; however, even the basics are here to serve as a reminder of what not to post. It's for your personal protection, your family's protection and for the protection of your future reputation.

If any of these bad examples look familiar, go into your profiles immediately to fix things. Your goal is to present a sparkling image to the world when it counts. Basically, you want to clean up and edit out (i.e., remove!) anything that resembles these from your pages and profiles right away.

Talking Trash

"If you can't say something nice, don't say anything at all." Talking trash about others or making rude comments about the places you visit or the people you meet needs to be addressed within your tweets and posts. What you think is funny can be damaging if misinterpreted or taken out of context. Don't come across as a jerk, bully or brat. Be nice.

Bad to the Bone

"OMG! I can't believe we did that!" Sure it may be fun and exciting when you and your friends perfect a stunt, pull a prank, break the law, and kick up crazy sometimes. Some may say that certain acts of criminal mischief (tagging or toilet-papering someone's house, for instance) are part of growing up. However, if those activities are illegal and/or dangerous, you need to remove the evidence. It's best not to boast about your bad behavior. Capturing those moments on places like Instagram may be fun to share – like when you're "king of the world" at the top of your city's water tower, spray painting a stop sign or highway bridge, camping out next to a no trespassing sign, or even throwing rocks at the vacant house hoping to break a window. However, posting evidence of such as behavior shows further bad judgment on your part. Not only were you dumb enough to do it… you also were dumb enough to share it with the world! It's best to save those memories without preserving them online. And it's even better to not to break the law to begin with.

Red Solo Cups

You may love to sing along to the Toby Keith party anthem "Let's have a party!" but those best receptacles are exactly what people who matter to your future do NOT want to see on the pages and posts of underage applicants. In fact, it's an unwritten rule of publicity and public relations to never be photographed with a drink in your hand, even if it's soda. People may not understand or appreciate the context of the photo (where it was taken, what was happening, the inside joke behind it, etc.) and that image might be used against you in their minds. Honestly, if you don't know a young person but you see a photo of them at a party holding a red Solo cup as they laugh and smile with their friends, you might assume they're enjoying some sort of alcohol. Those red party cups may not actually say the word "beer" or "cocktail" on them, but they might as well. Grownups were students once, too. Anyone who has gone to college and "lived the dream," (including those at the receiving end of your application) probably have an idea of what's going on. This is especially unfortunate if the person in the photo is under 21. College administrators have enough headaches with underage drinking on campus, so it's best to remove any photos that could lead someone to assume that your kind of fun usually includes partying. This also goes for beer pong practice. Even if the cups are filled with Sprite, and even if the parents are closely supervising the party, it just looks bad in the photos when posted online.

Weapons of Mass Consumption

Not only is underage drinking is a real problem, over-consumption is deadly serious. Do not post photos of you (or your friends) with a huge handle bottle of Jack… wearing hard-hats on game day that hold a beer on each side… and don't even get me started on beer bongs and keg stands. (You are not "Frank the Tank" from the movie "Old School.") The sober reality is that alcohol poisoning takes the lives of students every year. It's a complete tragedy for the school community and the families of those who go too far with their "fun." As impressive as you think your power-chug partying may be, get rid of those photos and stay safe. Know when to say when, and if you're under 21, stick with soda instead.

Let Me Be "Blunt"

Your pages should be a smoke-free environment. Even worse than underage drinking is any hint of illegal drug use among students. That means when you're at a party, be sure you're not pictured near someone with a hand-rolled tobacco blunt, a joint, a loud, a hookah, or any sort of other crack pipe. Drug use is illegal, so even if you are as clean and as straight as you can be, you don't want people to assume otherwise because of the company you keep. Consider it to be guilt by association. You also want to avoid posting photos where people are joking about actual drug use. Baggies of oregano, lines of sugar on a mirror or hookah filled with flavored tobacco can look just as incriminating as the real thing. No boss or admissions officer wants to give a break to someone who they believe could be a drug user. Simply don't share photos that have the potential of making you look bad. This includes anything that may imply you're not who you claim to be on the application or in the interview. Remember the SWAG Rules (page 13). Posting photos of drug use is almost always a bad idea, even if pot use is legal in your area. Cigarette smoking looks bad, too. In other words, thank you for not smoking.

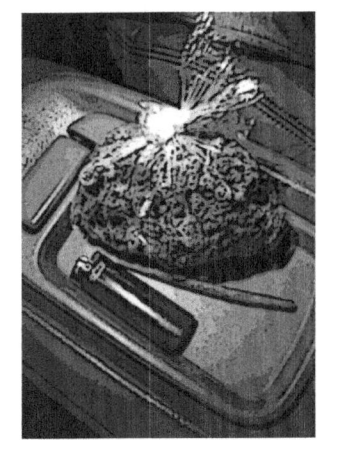

My So-Called Life

You may hate your life, but it's a good idea not to share that with the rest of the world on a frequent basis. If you're one of those people who use sarcasm and negativity as part of their humor, take a closer look at how it reads online. People who are checking you out online may not understand the context of your statement or the fact that you're using an ironic tone. Bitter is never attractive. Constantly complaining about how your family is lame, how stupid your summer vacation is, that your school is full of losers and you can't wait to graduate all makes you appear as if you have a darker side, one that may not be a good fit for the positive environment other people try to create, both at work and on campus. Of course, your comments need to be authentic. Blogging, tweeting and posting is a great way to share what you're feeling; just make sure that your pages and posts are not overwhelmingly negative. For every negative post, there should be at least two positive ones. You don't have to be a happy unicorn pooping sparkles and cupcakes all the time, but you don't want your sarcastic or snarky comments to overshadow what you do appreciate about your life. Don't let the dark days prevent your best self from shining through.

Nasty Sign Language

TEEN CHALLENGE

Actions often do speak louder than words – especially when you use your middle finger to "express" yourself. Other physical expressions captured in photos and posted online can also be in bad taste. Motioning to your crotch, making an obscene gesture toward others, making gang symbols (even as a joke) – all of these may be funny to you and your friends, but people who may be checking you out online may not find it funny at all. Don't assume they won't understand or know what it means. (It may be their job to know or to find out.) You're much better off removing the images of you and your friends signaling something naughty. Why risk it?

Your Birthday Suit

There are pictures of you having a blast, showing off your Twilight underpants or that daring itsy-bitsy string bikini. Be aware that showing too much skin in photos posted online is almost always a bad idea. Even if you think its fine to show off your new belly ring or the tattoo just below your hip, it may border on offensive to others. This also applies to all those boys who take mirror shots of their abs to show them off. Put your clothes back on. If you'd be embarrassed to show your grandmother that photo, it's best to not post it at all. And if you get tagged by others in any photo that shows you in a negative light, don't be afraid to ask the person posting the image to remove the reference to you or (better yet) have them delete the photo.

Pink Flamingos in the Pool

"It's a blacked out blur, but I'm pretty sure it ruled…" to quote Katy Perry. Let's just say the song "Last Friday Night (TGIF)" should not be your personal branding strategy when trying to impress for success. Alcohol and drug abuse is a huge concern for colleges and high schools. While it may be funny to post a photo of you totally wasted, passed out, or face first in a toilet waiting to throw up, it may not be so funny to other people who care about you and your success. In fact, that sort of behavior can be a nightmare. As mentioned earlier, students have died from alcohol poisoning, from choking in their own vomit. One night of fun can turn into a lifetime of sadness for their families. But why give people a reason to reject you in favor of another candidate, one who seems to have a squeaky clean image? Who would you rather have on your team... the person who was hung over and needs a nap, or the one who presents an image of self-control and confidence? If you have any party pictures of you glassy eyed and "not at your best" (or non-photogenic moments when you might look like that), it's best to remove those altogether from the Internet. You can't trust privacy settings to hide them for you. As anyone who has ever run for public office can tell you, bad photos and bad decisions seem to have a way of being discovered. Get rid of them now.

Bad Language

You may not give a _____ about what people think about the way you talk and the words you use, but people who matter certainly do care. Etiquette rules say "The use of profanity implies the lack of an adequate vocabulary." In fact, using profanity and inappropriate words in your social media posts says far more about you than the words on the page, and what it says about you may not be the story you want to tell. It would be a shame if you were disqualified from an opportunity for an F bomb. Abbreviations (WTF, LMFAO, etc.) aren't much better. It's time to go in and clean it up.

TMI on PDA

Love! It's so wonderful when you meet someone who is so special to you that you want the world to know how much you love them, want them, need them, crave them. However, there are some things that may be considered TMI (too much information) for you to share online. When it comes to PDA (public displays of affection), a picture of a peck on the cheek is sweet to share. Rubbing noses in an "Eskimo kiss" portrait is adorable. But it's just gross to go further than that in the photos you share with others through social media. Things NOT to post can include heavy kissing, groping, too much skin, and things that might make your grandmother blush. If you would be afraid or embarrassed about your family seeing the photos, you probably wouldn't want your future boss or program director to see them either. People might get the wrong idea about you. It is always best to keep private moments private.

Identity Details

Cybercrimes including identity theft are on the rise. Beware what you post online. There are bad people out there who scan social media sites to target individuals and their families. They look for opportunities to take advantage of people (perhaps people like you) who are naive and share too much information. Posting things like your address, phone number, date and year of birth, and even giving access to your Facebook account, isn't such a great idea. Don't be fooled – people are not who they claim to be, and they will try to exploit online relationships to gather information from you. Do you actually know every person who is a friend or follower? Are they actual friends or just people who sent you a friend request who you think you kind of know from someone you used to know? Be aware that people might use information from your Facebook profile to create another "you," stealing your identity and ruining your credit before you even land your first job. When it comes to sharing personal information online, less is always more.

False Friends

In August 2012, Facebook reported that 8.7 percent of profiles on the site are fake accounts. While 8.7 percent may not seem like a big number to you, it adds up to roughly 83 million fictitious users. With that in mind, it's important to know that not everyone who sends you a friend request is necessarily your friend. Just as it's easy for you to clean up your online identity, it's also easy for strange people to create completely fictitious identities, pretending to be someone they're not so they can take advantage of people. It's referred to as "catfishing." Be smart and selective about who you connect with online. Never make plans to meet someone who you only know through Facebook. Go through your friend lists and unfriend people you don't know personally and block people who seem creepy. Trust your gut. Chances are they won't find out you unfriended them, so don't worry about hurting their feelings or disappointing them. Your safety is more important, so don't take any chances. Be on guard for false friends.

Don't be a Hater

One sure way to learn about the character of a student is to see what they have to say on Twitter and Facebook. Don't come across as a hater. Making racist remarks, even when joking or quoting a song, reflects poorly on you. Sometimes it can be interpreted as hate speech. Most colleges and work environments support diversity and tolerance. Declaring your animosity and disdain for people because of their gender, age, weight, country of origin, religion, sexual orientation, or even their choice in clothing and hairstyle, can give others a reason to select someone else over you. Obviously any photos or posts that could be interpreted as mocking those who are different from you should be taken down right away. If you do want to be a hater, hate things that are worth hating. For instance, if you are vegan you might hate red meat. Or if you are interested in global conservation, you may hate deforestation. Or if you're an animal rights supporter, you may hate fur. Hate policies – not people. Sometimes there are good things to hate. Just be sure the negatives you share will put you in a positive light.

Avoid Controversy

If you're trying to get into a competitive school, earn a sports scholarship or be accepted into an exclusive program, you may want to think twice before posting things that may be perceived as overly controversial. Today's society is increasingly polarized, with people grouping into different camps of beliefs. Social media can be a hotbed of ideology, so tread carefully when you enter into debates. When you do, it's important that your views are reasonable and respectful, attacking the idea, not the person. If you see common ground or something you agree with, share that along with your objection. Not everyone who reads your pages and posts will agree with you, but they should be able to understand where you're coming from and appreciate the fact that you have an opinion on a topic – one that you can communicate respectfully. Use caution when your observations devolve into rants or heated rhetoric. Be aware that sex, politics, and religion are emotional topics and can spark more controversy than others. Be respectful and gracious when you choose to engage.

Stop Complaining

It's never a good idea to publicly complain at length about your teachers, your school, your coaches, and other people who have authority over you. This is what the expression "Never bite the hand that feeds you" is all about. Don't attack people who are there to help you – even if you feel it's justified. Whining about them just makes you look bad, not them. If you play a sport, it also is a bad idea to brutally criticize your opponents. Social media, while an excellent way to communicate thoughts and ideas, can often get people into hot water when criticism leads to controversy. Once you put something out there, it sometimes is hard to take back. Be nice, and if you haven't been nice in the past, now is a good time to edit out the negativity. The mirror reflects back on you.

A List of Don'ts, and other Best Practices

Don't make status updates at the wrong moments. For instance, don't share posts about the great day you're having at the amusement park when you're supposed to be home sick from school with the flu. And if you're not allowed to have your phones out during the school day, don't tweet during class when the timestamp on the post will give you away. School administrators and employers do monitor social activity (and time of posts) of students and staff, so don't give them a reason to suspend you (or fire you) over the bad timing of a tweet.

Don't make racist or hateful remarks. Also, don't make inappropriate or controversial comments that go against the values and policies of the school, team, and organization. Even if you think they'll never find out, there's always the chance that someone will bring it to their attention. (Even if you change the "er" to an "a," it's still not a good idea.)

Don't show too much skin. Nobody wants to see "all that." Think about what your grandma would be okay with if she saw what you were posting. Keep it clean.

Don't make threats over the Internet. This should go without saying, but what you think is funny or ridiculous can get you in trouble – or even in jail. Declaring you're going to blow up the tuba section of your high school band, or go "Aurora Colorado style" at the movies on Friday, or that you have a list of people you want to get rid of one by one... none of these things are funny at all. Authorities take matters of public safety very seriously. Causing alarm with a stupid comment or post will cause serious harm to your reputation – and quite possibly your future. Be smart.

Don't share confidential or sensitive information online. This can include private information about people, your teachers or your employers. For instance, if your parents are close friends with a teacher and you find out she's going to rehab over Winter Break, you don't need to broadcast that information on Facebook. If you work at a major retailer and you know they're starting their Black Friday sale at noon on Thanksgiving Day, that is competitive corporate information and should not be shared. Being able to uphold a confidence and keep a secret shows that you are a person of integrity who can be trusted. People don't like to do business with people they don't trust. Always be virtuous. (If you don't know what that word means, please look it up.)

Don't make fun of other people. Stop pointing out the weaknesses and failings of others. Nobody likes a bully and you will be sure that what you say to mock other people or as a joke online may come back to haunt you. In fact, it could rob you of opportunities that should be yours when your statements come off as being cruel.

Security Concerns

In addition to catfishing, there are other safety concerns. Years ago, criminals used the death notices and obituaries to see when families would be out of the house, attending the funeral of a loved one. Today they use Facebook, scanning posts about upcoming vacations, plus personal details to use to steal your identity. Don't make it easy for predators to take advantage of you, or (worse yet) harm your family members. Don't offer details of your life and schedule such as "I can't wait – my parents are taking me to Disney World in June!" or "Saturday morning starts my week at the beach!" or "I can't believe we have to go all the way to Iowa for my grandma's funeral." It's best not to share the dates and times of when you leave and when you'll be back. Post those trip photos after you return.

Be smart about what you share online.

Never post the following online:

1) Your birth date and place of birth
2) Your mother's maiden name
3) Your home address
4) The fact that you're not home
5) Specific locations where others can find you
6) Incriminating photos (Even Snapchat stores images for a period of time.)
7) Illegal activities (The police will find you.)
8) Your phone number (Even for the "I lost my phone and all my contacts" requests.)
9) Countdown to vacations or to the beach
10) Children's names (including your siblings' identities, tagged in photos)
11) The inside of your home and its valuables

Cyber-Bullying, Shunning and More

With all the talk about cyber bullying and all the discussion about showing kindness to others through your words and posts, you need to understand that the victim of bullying online is not just the person targeted. The real loser is the person who made those comments in the first place. Even if you don't buy into the whole "peace, love, and acceptance" ideas, your actions, such as making fun of others through social media, certainly increase the likelihood of your future failure because of your cruelty today.

Nobody likes a bully. More important is the fact that nobody wants to help or hire a bully. Being unkind others can directly impact your future opportunity, especially when people are victimized as a result of what you do online.

Frankly, even a share of something that could be considered cyber bullying makes you look bad for even participating in the thread. When social media conversation takes an ugly turn, or when you are aware that someone is being attacked online, the best thing you can do is to help. Find a way to interject some positivity. Stand up for the person who is the target of the attack. Be the defender of the meek. Show your support and compassion. If things go too far, go tell a teacher or counselor about it. Not only will you make a difference in someone else's life, you'll also shine as someone who has the leadership to stand up for others. Do the right thing.

Why Your Posts Matter

As colleges sort through thousands of applications and companies sort through mountains of resumes for a single job opening, you can be busy online making sure you stand out from the crowd. Just because you see yourself as the star of your team, popular or someone who deserves a break, without a thoughtful approach to social media, you might become your own worst enemy. Your lack of personal brand management could work against you and sabotage your goals and dreams, one post at a time. You may not even realize it when it happens. Employers and admissions people will find some other excuse to exclude you from consideration instead telling you what they found when searching you online.

It's best to take a proactive approach, to clean up your image, and have a plan for the type of person you want to project to others online – your best self. Now is the time to do what is necessary to put yourself in a good position so when opportunities come up, you're perceived as the best possible candidate. All it takes is a little bit of planning to make sure your best self shines with authenticity and joy.

Leading a Double Life

Some students think it's a good idea to have two different online accounts for social media – one for fun and one to share with recruiters. This is not recommended. Having a second profile and only sharing the first is kind of like cheating on your spouse – leading a double life and hiding the person you truly are. Be aware that in today's transparent "big data" world, it's tough to do or say anything online that's not traceable or available to be discovered if the person knows where to dig. Plus, your "good side" may not get the level of posts and activity as your "bad side" which means it's possible that your bad side will rank higher in search.

Communicating online is like living in a glass house. You may put up drapes and curtains to protect outsiders from seeing what you do, but there will always be that chance (with increasing likelihood) that people will see right through to what's really happening. With all the recent advancements such as automated photo face recognition tools, tagging by friends and family who don't know the right name to use, gathering of online data by digital media companies to track your activity down to the individual (like when you log in using your Facebook account), you're far better off sticking to a single persona and making it fabulous. Plus, explaining the reason for both (once the second "you" is discovered) is quite awkward. You don't want to go there. It just looks bad, as if you have something serious to hide. You could come across as trying to cheat the system, which is also bad. A second identity just isn't worth it.

Time to Get Busy

For most college-bound students, chances are you've already have a life on the Internet. Now that you have the information on how to use social media to your advantage, it's time to do something with it. For starters, explore your existing presence online. Review the information in this chapter and remove (right away, please) the posts and images from your pages and walls to help clean up your image. Do what you need to do in order to create an online reputation that's truly worthy of the bright future that you deserve.

A Note for Protective Parents

Hello parents! There may be some of you who want to protect your children from the so-called perils of social media. Maybe some who read this book have already decided that allowing their child to use social media is too risky. They would rather them not have a Twitter or Facebook or Instagram account at all, instead of risking the chance that something bad could happen and their reputation be harmed.

Better to not do anything at all, right? Wrong! This is a terrible mistake for parents to make. The adoption rate of social media and digital communications is significant among young people. Having the skills and experience – and using it in the correct way – is a real bonus to future employers and schools. It's almost a basic expectation for today's generation to understand how to use online channels. If they do not have your permission to join in to social media conversations or to share their ideas in 140 characters or less, it just makes it that much harder for them to create a positive personal brand later. Online branding takes time, so their lack of involvement puts them behind the rest. Friends at school will still post, tweet and tag pictures of your child online. People will still comment about activities and events that involve your children. These comments and inclusions should not go unanswered. I believe that it's better for young people to be active and engaged, to use the tools available to them, especially when they use them strategically. Reading this book is a good place to start. With the right information, understanding and trust, your child can get a real advantage. Plus, your son or daughter can make a wonderful difference within their group of friends in the ideas they share and the positive things they post. Give them permission to shine. Make it easy for them to shape their identity online without fear – and without going behind your back. It's important to "plant the garden" of a positive personal brand than later deal with the weeds that will show up because of an absence of activity online.

The decision is up to you. There are things you can do to help protect and monitor your child online, such as installing spyware on phones and computers, installing security software to block inappropriate websites, making sure you have all passwords to each social media account they use, requiring them to "friend" you on Facebook and following them on Twitter. Of course, do what you think is best for your child. Giving them the right guidance (like this book and the corresponding in-school program, coming soon) and having a little trust can go a long way to their success and happiness. For more tips, news, and tools, visit www.WhatNot2Post.com.

Your Online Reputation

Picture a plot of fresh dirt, ready to be tilled and planted. The soil is rich, just begging for roots to take hold. Your online reputation is like that fresh soil. Something is going to plant itself there and grow eventually. It's up to you to decide what seeds take hold. Do you ignore it and let the weeds take over? Or do you decide to take the time to work the soil of your reputation, planting page after page with positive items – ones that will take root, flower and bear fruit? It's up to you to decide the image that grows.

Because you are the gardener of your online image, it's your job to tend to your crops. Is there a weed somewhere that needs pulled, like being tagged in a bad photo? Get rid of it so better posts can take its place. You can control the first impression others have of you when they search you online. Will they see a gorgeous array of flowers with rich blossoms and strong roots, or just a bunch of crabgrass?

Everybody has an online reputation. If yours is good, bad or even non-existent, it still says something about you. Lots of information about you (and especially the wrong type) can be bad, but so can a complete lack of information. You do not live in a void, so your online persona should not be empty either. If you appear to be a ghost online, it could leave the impression that you're not involved, not connected, or hiding something.

For those interested in learning the back story about you, studies show they turn to the Web. Because people who matter are checking you out online first, your job is to manage the information they see.

As you develop your personal brand online, consider your audience. What is it you're trying to achieve? What are your goals? Who can help you get there – and what do they want to know most about you?

When planting this online garden of yours, let's walk through some of the things that blossom best.

Too often people use their social media activity as a diary, recording every thought, each activity or each emotion that sweeps over them. I call this Facebook Therapy – using social media to vent your frustrations. Twitter Tales are much the same, tweeting every action and opinion as you navigate your day. But if you're interested in designing a successful online brand for yourself, you must resist doing this. As mentioned earlier, the Internet can often act as a mirror – your activity, posts and comments offer a digital reflection of you for the world to see. Even though you think you're alone in your room, sharing with your friends, you're really not. With each keystroke, you are building your image.

Just the other day, I was talking with a friend of mine who is nationally known for mentoring CEOs and women leaders. She told me about her new client. When she went to find out more about this new person online, she discovered that according to her social media posts, the woman "can't stop eating jelly beans," to which my friend replied, "I don't really need to know that about her. It makes me question working with her." It seems this person's online persona was filled with random reflections with almost nothing about her career, her ambitions, her expertise or her success. My friend walked away unsure about whether this woman would be worth her time to mentor. This shows that even adults get it wrong sometimes. So, the sooner you figure out how to lead the social conversation and how to create a positive online reputation, the sooner people like Miss Jelly Bean will be working for you.

Think of your online image as a mosaic. Mosaics are pieces of art where the image is created from a large number of smaller pieces or tiles. All of those tiny colorful pieces make up the stunning walls at the Taj Mahal and even in the New York subways. A clean background is peppered with patterns of colored tiles to create a masterpiece. Each tiny square is strategically placed, part of a larger canvas to communicate the broader image. When you hold one little piece of tile, it seems insignificant – but add it to the design with hundreds of other tiny pieces and you can see the image begin to take shape.

These tiny tiles are much like your tweets and posts over time. Each one may seem harmless enough, but over time they can accumulate to create your online image. Your digital self-portrait is created from all the bits of information that's out there about you. You are the creator. You have control over the design your pieces (comments) take.

With that in mind, let's look at some favorite topics to post that will reflect the true you, at your best.

What to Post

Your Amazing Talents

Everyone has something they love to do, something to be proud of. Show what you're great at – your unique gifts and abilities. Maybe you're awesome at free throws. Maybe you love to play the guitar, or you're in the marching band. That photo of you at the football game rocking your tuba, or on stage at the talent show, on the basketball court lining up for your shot is exactly the type of thing people like to see. Accentuate the positive. Show off your strengths. Share your enthusiasm about the things you love to do – what you're good at. "Can't wait to _____ (dance/sing/play/compete)!" is just one way to start the conversation about what you do best, without coming off as boastful or too confident.

Your Team Together

Go ahead and put that group photo of you and your teammates out there. This shows that you're a team player. So what if you're not a superstar! Colleges and employers want to see that you work well with others. Sharing a team photo accomplishes a couple positives. It shows that you can contribute to a group, that you play well with others and you're not afraid to get involved. When people are doing their homework on you (and they will), show them you can place the group (your team) before your own individual interests. Share how your assists or support helped contribute to the overall team success – which is a great quality for students to share.

Your Artistic Genius

Sharing your own artwork in posts is a good way to show others that there's more to you than what meets the eye. If you're interested in a career in art or design, this is a no-brainer. You should have a mini-gallery or portfolio of your work online to share with recruiters and the like. But even if you have no interest in pursuing art, sharing your creative abilities shows you're a well-rounded person with many talents. It also shows confidence. Plus, studies have found that people who can express themselves creatively have strong critical thinking abilities. Things like posters, banners, web pages, invitations, memes, and other projects are good to post. Things like graffiti or designs that feature rough language (swear words, etc.) are best not to post.

Your High Notes

Music ability is a great thing to share via social media – and it's something that will reverberate in good ways with colleges. Share photos of you rocking it out with your band... singing with the choir... in step with the marching band... strumming your guitar with friends at the park. Music takes practice, which proves you can stick with something. Being part of a music group also takes teamwork and cooperation. Plus, people love to see photos and posts of you entertaining others with your gifts. And when you make it big, you'll give your friends more reason to say "I knew them when...."

Your Best Dressed

Whether you arrive Gangnam style in a bright yellow suit for Homecoming or in a blue tuxedo for your cousin's wedding, photos of you at formal dances and events posted on Facebook or Instagram highlight another positive side of you. It shows you clean up well, that you're willing to make the effort to look good and have a great time. Even if no one could teach you how to Dougie, even the more awkward photos are worth sharing. Most people have memories of anxious school dance moments, so sharing family photos from weddings, proms and formal fun helps admissions officers and potential employers get a glimpse of someone (you!) they, too, can relate to – they've been there themselves. Share the joy of those moments in your posts.

Your Outdoor Fun

Ah, the great outdoors! If you love to get outside and enjoy the gifts of Mother Nature, share some of those moments online. Ski clubs, hiking sprees, camping... Show your love of nature with posts of activities that take you beyond your couch and classroom. Colleges love young people who are passionate about the environment, who have an interest in sustainability and wildlife preservation. If this truly matters to you, be sure to share, to let people know. Not only can you post photos of you and your friends having fun, or places of true beauty – you also can show your affiliation with groups who share your same interests with your likes, posts and pins.

Your Wild Destinations

There's a big world out there just waiting to be explored! Travel photos show that you have experiences and interests beyond the borders of your hometown. If you're interested in a specific college, be sure to check out their mission statements and the qualities they're looking for in their students. Some indicate a desire for "global awareness" or an appreciation for people of all cultures and nations. Of course, if you don't have your passport and opportunity to jet set is limited, you can always show your understanding and love of other cultures with pins and posts of places you'd love to go, and share a comment why. Things like links from foreign media, images of places you plan to visit, photos of friends you meet from other countries or cultures, etc. show that you have an appreciation that spans beyond where you are today. And if the campus is culturally diverse, they may be interested to see that you'll be able to enjoy and enhance their university community.

Your Curtain Call

One way to take center stage with positive first impressions is to show off your involvement in theater. It's an extracurricular activity that colleges love to see because it shows that you can put in the extra hours at long practices, work well with a group, take instruction, memorize the written word and interpret it for stage, speak clearly with confidence, stay focused, and handle being in front of an audience. All of these experiences benefit the college-bound student, so if you've had a role in live theater, post those pictures and share your success. (Chorus counts, too.) And if you're too shy for the spotlight, you can still be part of the theater family and help with set construction, props, costumes, and more. But not matter how you get involved, share the moments of fun with others.

Your Teen Spirit

Even if you hate that old Nirvana song, there is something to be said for people who are passionate about their school team and classmates. Showing your school spirit can be as simple as wearing a letter/school jacket, face painting before the big game, or doing goofy cheers with your friends. Colleges and future employers like people who are spirited, who show they can be both loyal and enthusiastic to bring a positive energy to the place. It also shows you actually go to the games and activities, and take part in the old-fashioned healthy fun that life has to offer. College is loaded with opportunity to continue that game-day joy. Show you know how to root, root, root your fellow students on to success. Share those posts and photos. People love to see them.

Your Best

Those sweet moments when you break through and achieve success on the court, ring, rink or field are excellent to share. It's hardly luck. In order to achieve those great moments, a person needs discipline to their sport, and a focus toward their personal goals to achieve excellence. In a world where it seems like everybody gets a trophy just for being on the team, your strength in the sport of choice should be celebrated. Part of developing a personal brand that sticks in people's minds (those you hope to positively impress) is showing why you stand out from the rest of the pack. Your super-star moments – that glorious catch in the end zone, perfect slam dunk, clearing that hurdle, spiking over the net – are ideal to show you already have the burning desire for excellence. And if you're hoping to be recruited for college sports and scholarships, a few extra shots of your best moments can't hurt. (Be careful not to overdo it and look like you're a fan club of one.) If you don't have your own photos, check with your mom, dad, coaches or even the sports photographers for the local news.

Your Not-So-Best

Not everyone can be the best at everything all the time. Those moments of trial and error – especially the errors – can be good to post to show a balanced perspective of your trials on the field, court, track, rink, etc. As great as it is to share the "money shots," it's also good to season your pages with a few bloopers – things you might laugh about later. Maybe you tripped at track or face-planted diving into third, missing the base. Nobody's perfect, and showing you have a sense of humor with a hint of self-deprecation can be endearing. It also helps balance your posts so they don't come across as pure shameless self-promotion. Keep it real.

Your Awards and Honors

Recognition can be a beautiful thing. You should be proud of your accomplishments. Your blue ribbon at the art show... your runner-up for best jam at the county fair... your medal for best sportsmanship... best costume... spirit awards... all these things are great to share with posts and photos. Of course you don't want to list every last honor on your college applications or job resumes, but these are nice things to feature as an element of your online persona. It reinforces your capability for success, that there's more to you than your SAT scores or work history. Setting up a photo gallery on Facebook filled with images of your recognitions may be worth doing.

Your Leadership

Your leadership roles are great things to talk about in posts. It shows that you have valuable skills employers and colleges look for, so these are important to share. This extends beyond the obvious student government roles. It can encompass far more activities – even those outside of school. Some suggestions: chairman of a fundraiser at school or church; section leader in the band or choir; youth leader at your church; captain of your debate team; editor of the school newspaper; committee leader for a political campaign or cause, and so on. Leadership is certainly something to include in your personal branding mix of topics.

Your Kindness to Others

Simple acts of helping as a mentor can reveal what type of person you are. Think about what you're good at, or what matters to you so much that you're willing to take the time to share with others. Things like tutoring math to others during study hall, or volunteering to read to children at the local library, helping as a host guide for new students, or being a CIT or counselor at summer camp – all will help build a positive image in the eyes of others. Plus they're fun! But it's important to be authentic in what you do. Don't do it just to build a better application – do it because it matters to you, then share what a difference it makes to you (as well as to others) in your posts.

Your Community Service

There is an old saying, "You keep only what you give away." That means there's real value in giving your time in the service to others. This especially applies to good works in your community. It doesn't have to be a mission trip (though those make great photo opportunities). Many schools expect a number of community service hours before graduation, and that's good to share. But it's even better when the desire to serve comes from you – because you want to, not because you have to. Maybe you like to help hand out water to marathon runners, or serve up soup at the hunger shelter, or hold up poster signs for the team car wash, or shovel snow from your elderly neighbor's sidewalk. Your good works that have a positive impact on your community can make excellent posts. You don't have to always include photos – just sharing your actions in updates can inspire others to do more of the same. It also will go a long way in creating an authentic, positive image while making your world a better place.

Your Science Fairs and Mathletes

 Colleges want to know what you're good at – what you love to do – and that includes your excellence in math and science. It's impressive if you can build a rocket ship out of Mentos and tin foil, or that you placed 2nd in the math competition. Celebrate your inner geek and share some of it in your posts. You may be cooler than you think – and colleges love to see what you can do. Such competitions help showcase your best work.

Your Creative Talents

If you got up your nerve enough and put yourself out there to be in a talent show, art contest or writing competition, share your great work with a post or two. Video of you hitting your high note, excerpts of your poetry, photos of your art – all are great things to share to show you're not only talented, you're also confident in your abilities. Shine bright and share it.

Your Groups and Gatherings

It's fun to belong. When you come together with others who share a common interest, good things can happen. Extracurricular clubs and societies can show you have interests beyond your classroom – that you want to go further in that area. Share your involvement, what you do and what it means to you. Our activities and efforts shape who we may someday become, so it's a great things to post. It also shows you have the ability to commit and work for a common goal when it's not for a grade or to fulfill a requirement. That's a good thing for recruiters to see. Be advised that it's better to go deep and spend more time in limited number of clubs than spread yourself too thin across too many groups.

Your Hard Work

Everyone loves a self-starter, someone who displays a strong work ethic and commitment to personal success. If you're lucky enough to land an internship or even a part-time job, post about what you love to do there and the things you learn. Even the lowliest jobs can be valuable in the minds of recruiters and admissions folks. Fast food work teaches efficiency and shows your ability to follow a system and follow instruction. Waiters and waitresses learn selling skills and how to deal with all different types of people. Administrative work shows an attention to detail and organizational skills. All these things can give you an edge when it matters.

Your Friendships and Fun

Showcase your friendships, capture the fun, and surround yourself with people who will lift you up – not hold you back. Remember, you are the sum of the people you're closest to. Think about that – who are you close to? Who shows up on your pages? Unfortunately in some cases you can be guilty by association. If your group photos are with people who look like thugs, druggies or wild ones, think about whether or not this looks like "you." (Is that the image you're trying to put out there?) Recruiters who use Facebook will dig into friend photos. Be sure to build your online community around what's positive.

Your Hobbies and Passions

That burning desire and interest you have about specific topics should be shared. What do you love? What makes you, well, you? If you love fashion, post things about the looks you love or comment on the latest trends. If you love gardening, share your enthusiasm that your orchid is blooming. If you love a specific genre of music, let your likes tell that story. Let your social activity communicate a picture of who you are, and what matters most.

Your Family Fun

You probably have hundreds of photos of birthday parties, trips, weddings, holidays, and family dinners. A healthy family with strong relationships is a positive thing to share. Even if you think your family is lame, show how they put the "fun" in "dysfunctional." Sharing images of your family connections – of you being a helpful big sister or kind big brother – gives a glimpse that you might get along well with your freshman year roommate, and that you're capable of having good relationships with others. Sharing the love – and the love you have for your family – can never be a bad thing.

Clean Up Your Act

NOTE: This is not how to clean your image. (Do not attempt.)

DISCLAIMER: The images used throughout this book were purchased or free stock photography, or they were photos accessed due to weak privacy settings on Facebook accounts, considered public information.

Details on updating your photo privacy settings are in the pages to follow.

10-Step Social Media Checklist

Think before you post, and then double-check everything.

In addition to the SWAG Rules mentioned earlier, quality of posts also matters. When you're using social media activities to support a specific online image you want for yourself, consider the following checklist before you decide to update or tweet.

1) *WIIFM: What's in it for me?* – Does sharing this idea, link or detail help move you closer to your goals or priorities? Consider the four Fs: Fun, Friends, Family, and Future. If it showcases any of these areas in a positive light, go for it! And if not (like if you're making fun of someone or you're mad at your mom), maybe you're better off not sharing after all – especially if it could reflect negatively on you.

2) *Will anyone care?* – Who is the audience for this post (your friends, recruiters, future employers, family, etc.) and is this interesting or desirable to them? Is it sharing something they can take action on? Does it add value, or is it just filling up space on the page? Keep your goals in mind, but always be authentic.

3) *Is it actually true?* – If the information you're sharing doesn't show someone or something in a positive light (people you know, your school, an event, etc.), is the

information fairly reported and accurate? If you're just not sure, don't retweet, share or expand what could be misleading or incorrect. If it's a lie, let it die.

4) *Is it too extreme?* – Does it endorse or support a certain political or religious view or ideology? If it does, take an extra look at what you're saying so it isn't later viewed as being extreme or offensive. Yes, stay true to who you are, but you can do so without being provocative and causing controversy. And if you do choose to get people riled up about a topic, be sure you're ready and informed enough to manage the threads and threats intelligently.

5) *Do your links work?* Don't get bit by bit.ly. If you're using a shortened URL for a link, make sure it works. Even though everyone has links blow out on Twitter sometimes, it doesn't have to happen to you. This makes you look like an amateur or that you don't pay attention to detail. Click and confirm first.

6) *Did ewe cheque grammer end spelling?* – Double check for spelling, grammar and format before you post. That means things like spacing between letters, the spelling of names, and using the correct variation of "sound alike" words. Of course shortened slang versions of common phrases are used all the time – those aren't the issue. The problem comes when you screw up things like "their, there, they're" consistently without realizing it. Yes, it matters.

7) *Is it tagged properly?* – When you use images or photos, is there anyone you should tag or mention? Did you use proper hashtags to make it easier for people to follow and find you?

8) *Are you sharing too much information?* – Privacy settings aside, social media can be like a catalog for criminals trying to target individuals. Something as simple as "Can't wait to go to

FL with the folks this weekend. We leave Friday!" can be an invitation to burglars to stop by while you're away. No one needs to know details that are sexual, gross, illegal or just TMI in general.

9) *Is it shameless self-promotion versus good news to share?* – It's one thing to share cool stuff going on in your life, but be careful not to overdo it. Make sure your posts are true to yourself – even those intended to put you in a positive light. A quick ego check doesn't hurt to make sure you present a balanced (not boastful) image.

10) Is this the image you want to present? This sums it up quite nicely. Confirm it's the image you wish to share with the world, especially if it leaks beyond your privacy settings (which will happen).

Other Tips

Fail fast, and fix it faster – if you've made a mistake, own up to it. Apologize for it. Make a correction quickly to minimize the issue. How you handle the fail reflects your character, and (as you've heard before) Character Counts. Admissions folks and recruiters care less that you made a mistake; they're more impressed that you dealt with it well.

Know how to love – Social media opens the conversation on lots of topics. Bad comments happen. People will be rude. Respond to the haters, but do it with love. That means you don't attack the person – you only attack or address their comment. Stick to your principles, but do so with some class.

Use common sense for your sense of humor – Not everyone agrees about what's funny or not. In fact, a joking comment to one person between friends can quickly devolve into the police at your door. Be smart about the things you share and comment. Consider if they could be read the wrong way or misinterpreted by others. If there's a chance, perhaps find a way to reword things. It's a shame when good fun turns into bad fallout. References to drug use and violent acts – even if you're joking – should be used with caution, if used at all. Of course, there's a right place and a right time for edgy humor. Just be sure those boundaries are clear between your funny commentary and your actual beliefs.

Timing is everything – A sophomore got an in-school suspension for sending a tweet. She didn't say anything bad. It was a nice comment, actually. Trouble was that her high school does not allow students to use social media during class ("No phones visible during class. Period.") While the teacher didn't see her, the assistant principal did. He quietly follows many of the students and saw her post at 9:42 a.m. – right in the middle of her History class. Moral of the story: There's a time and a place for everything; during class is not the time to be posting or tweeting. If you use HootSuite or other scheduling tools, make the school aware, especially if they have strict policies on this.

Personal Brand Management

You can't always control what people might say or post about you online, but you can control how easy it is to find the bad things out there. This requires you to be proactive in what you share, who can access it, and how you deal with items that are posted beyond your control, which could impact you negatively. If you've ever been tagged in a post or photo that you really didn't want to be associated with, you understand how both awkward and important this may be.

Reputation management begins with a typing your name and its variations into search engines. Start with Google, and then do the same with Bing, Yahoo, Ask, and any other search tools available. Also, go to the various social media sites and search there too. Be sure to "sign out" first so you can experience the results others do.

You'll be surprised at the random details that come up when you search for yourself. You also might be surprised that there are other people in the world with your same name who show up in results as well. These "other you's" are why it's so important to be purposeful when managing your online reputation or personal brand. With a focused effort on creating positive content through your posts, you can improve the page ranking of the real you and organically rise above the others in the search engines.

In some cases, this can be difficult, especially if you share the same name as a celebrity or other news maker. When this happens, do your best to adopt another relevant term along with your name that identifies you as unique – and separates you from that famous person. Perhaps it's your name with your hometown, or your name with the name of your school. Here's an example. Chris Brown is a terrific marketing professional. She was on Twitter and was blogging from the very start, well before the other Chris Brown became popular. But because of his success, she has had to add more description to her name to make sure her personal brand is not obfuscated (or hidden) by the famous singer's online persona. You may have to do the same. It starts with a search.

Manage your Settings

An important part of personal brand management is privacy. It is recommended that you update your privacy settings – especially for your photos on Facebook. Here's how you do it:

1) Log into Facebook.

2) Click on the account link on the upper right corner of the page.

3) Click on "Privacy Settings" in the drop-down options. The Privacy Setting page lets you manage who gets to see what images. The Facebook default allows everyone to have access to everything that you share on the site. You can change that to "Friends Only" or even tighter controls. To manage your photos, click on the "Custom" option, then click on "Customize Settings" (toward the bottom of the list of options).

4) On the Custom Settings page, you can dig in and manage your settings. At the bottom of the first section is the link "Edit privacy settings for existing photo albums and videos." Click on the link to go to the page where you can control access to images you've already posted.

5) Once you're on the page of your existing pictures and videos, you can go through and decide privacy settings for each album. Keep in mind that good photos are worth sharing, so you may not want to block every single image.

Social media is meant for sharing. Sharing is good. But sharing is better when you take a proactive approach to who gets to see what of your images online. Use your best judgment, the advice in this book, and even more suggestions at www.whatnot2post.com.

Create a Roadmap for Your Reputation

When creating a positive image of yourself online, it helps to have a specific plan in place to help you get started. Having a plan also gives you some guardrails, to keep you on the road to success – or at least moving in the right direction. Businesses call this "Reputation Management." Many of the same principles can apply to you. The exercises from earlier in the book can be applied here.

• Start with a blank piece of paper. Define who you are, or refer to the previous exercise. Then look to your future self and see if you know who you want to become someday. Create a vision for your future with as much detail as possible. It's just a piece of paper. Use words or pictures or doodles to fill the page with a definition of your best self.

• Review you specific goals and see how you can ensure your best self shines through your activity on social media. No need to make sweeping changes. Simply establish your goals, then see how your online activity can help support your journey to achieve them. Start with the end in mind, then think about things you can do and share to help move you toward that image in the eyes of others.

• Define what makes you unique that you'd like other people to better understand. What are your gifts? When people first meet you, what impression do you want them to walk away with after spending some time getting to know you?

• Connect with those with similar goals, interests and ideas to create a network. Social media is all about, well, being social. If you want to be a biomedical engineer like Mary, post some things related to that goal. Join groups. Like memes and other images that share your passions and interests. Be engaged.

• Monitor your online personal brand. Start with Google. Search your name and see what comes up. If you're serious about your online reputation and establishing a personal brand online, with a little effort the first three or four pages of a Google search under your name should be all about you. Contributing to forums, writing blog posts, publishing articles and other content, and especially your social media activity (especially when positive) can go a long way in giving you a commanding presence online – using social media to get ahead.

For ideas, news and examples on developing a personal brand online including best (and worst) practices for students using social media, check out:

Website: **www.whatnot2post.com**

Fan Page: **www.facebook.com/whatnot2post**

Twitter: **@WhatNot2Post**

CPSIA information can be obtained at www.ICGtesting.com
Printed in the USA
LVOW01s1628010813

345835LV00022B/1099/P